Meg

A PLAY IN THREE ACTS

by

Paula A. Vogel

Presented at the Ninth Annual American College Theatre Festival in Washington, D.C., as winner in the national competition for the Festival's Student Playwriting Award.

SAMUEL FRENCH

FOUNDED 1830

New York Hollywood London Toronto

SAMUELFRENCH.COM

Descriptive Story of the Play

The background to *Meg*, based on the life of
Margaret More Roper, is Tudor England, with its
political and ruthless male hierarchies of Henry VIII
and the Catholic Church. These are the offstage forces
imprisoning Meg, a unique woman isolated from her
time and environment through the gift and curse of
her developed intellect. As a play, *Meg* invites di-
rectors and casts with strong theatrical imaginations
to tackle the blend of direct-audience address, char-
acter transformations, intense two-person scenes and
lyrical language. The play intertwines several themes
and levels: on one level we see the story of Sir Thomas
More at a 180° perspective through his daughter's
eyes. It is also a story of a young female scholar's
education in the restraints of her roles of wife and
mother. It is, as well, an exploration of the father-
daughter relationship at that painful transition "when
father and daughter turn round and see each other as
man and woman." And, Meg Roper discovers, "Both
diminish in size." *Meg* is not a history play; it is a
play about history—which has been a history of omis-
sion as far as women are concerned. In this play,
interwoven with kings, popes and matters of state are
marriages, miscarriages, knittings before the fire, and
childhood reveries. Five characters, in three acts.

DESCRIPTION OF CHARACTERS
(in order of appearance)

MEG—a young woman of 18, of ordinary appearance —but mischievous, at times lively, at times reflective. Her costume is modest, but graceful.

SIR THOMAS MORE—middle-aged, slight of stature, scrawny in build, with thin pathetic legs in stockings which bag—and a look of mild embarrassment on his face. Rather shabbily dressed, his clothes usually sport the crumbs from his last meal.

CROMWELL—a pleasant looking middle aged man, also slight in stature; perhaps a bit portly. Dressed in expensive cloth of dark blues and violets.

WILLIAM ROPER—a young, juvenilely attractive "Village Idiot," age 18–22. He has a slight stammer, which improves by Act III. In Acts I and II, he wears rustic peasant clothes and boots, hat, and jacket. His court clothes (Acts II and III) are brilliant in hue, flashy and slightly foppish.

ALICE MORE—a plump, middle-aged housewife, dressed in practical gown with an apron containing ample folds and pockets, in which are tucked her constant companions—knitting and a rosary.

Meg

ACT ONE

*The stage consists of slightly raised platforms in a
variety of geometrical shapes and angles. In the
center of the stage, at a lower level than surround-
ing platforms, there is a rough wooden table, and
two chairs. Downstage left is a low, sawed-off
spherical monkey bar. On the top level are three
suggested locales—the Tower, stage right, suggested by a suspended arch and textures of iron
and chain; the chapel, stage left, with a metal
cross suspended beneath a gothic arch, and finally,
center, the More household, suggested by white,
rough plaster textures and heavy beams. In front
of the More house, there is a bench, and upon the
bench we see Alice More, a plump middle aged
housewife, who energetically "plucks" a chicken—
we see feathers fly from her apron.*

*Downstage, enmeshed in the monkey bars, we see
William Roper, a young, juvenilely attractive
"Village Idiot." Entangled in the structure, he
"moons" in the direction of the More household.*

*Mid-stage, seated at the table, scratching his legs and
simultaneously munching a muffin, is Sir Thomas
More, entranced in the reading of a book.*

*And stage right, in front of the Tower a pleasant look-
ing middle aged Cromwell sits upon the block,*

5

his hand absently fondling an axe handle which stands upright in the wood. Swinging his foot, he casually cleans his nails with a pen knife.

MARGARET MORE, *a young woman of 18, stands by the table holding aloft an enormous leather-bound book, a mock-solemn look upon her face. She gazes at the audience, and waits for our undivided attention. Then she begins to read:*

MEG. "Margaret More Roper was born in 1508, the beloved daughter of the reverent Saint Thomas More, martyr of the true Church—and died the obedient wife of William Roper, Esquire. Her renown as a scholar of Greek and Latin under her father's tutelage, unusual then as now to the female condition, was restrained and surpassed by a greater modesty becoming to her sex. She submitted her brilliance in all things to her father and husband, thereby increasing her lustre; and remains an example among women— as befits the daughter of a saint—saintly in compassion, humility, and obedience." (MEG *beams modestly at the audience as she slams the book shut.*) That's me—"saintly in compassion, humility, and obedience." Why, I've been saintly for over 400 years— Brigades of Catholic historians have rhapsodized over the remains of my reputation. Four hundred years of sermonizing and reproach to wives, mistresses, mothers, and school girls. (*Airily.*) Margaret the Modest, Margaret the Meek, Margaret the Mild. . . . (*Cynically.*) Margaret the Masochist— (MEG *stops herself. Then, continuing.*) There's not much else written about my life's story—but then, you have probably heard or read the other story—yes, you know the one—the story of my father's life. (MEG *turns towards him; seeing him occupied, she says gently:*) We'd best not disturb him right now. You know him as Sir Thomas More, the great writer of *Utopia*, and martyr to the Catholic Church. As chancellor to King Henry the VIII, he refused to acknowledge England's separation from Rome, and so was beheaded in . . . (MEG *searches her memory.*) 1535. (*Simply.*) A most regretable incident in English history. (MEG *glances over her shoulder at* CROMWELL.) Over there is the man who neatly engineered my father's decapitation— That is Master Thomas Cromwell, a man who replaced my father as chancellor to the king . . . one instance in which the rat followed the sinking ship— (MEG'S *glance rests on* WILL; *smiling.*) And down there is my future husband William Roper. The world remembers him as a pious, earnest man, who passed on the story of Thomas More's martyrdom—that is how the world remembers him. (MEG *pauses.*) Perhaps, as unwilling schoolchildren, captive in a sunny classroom, you have heard or read of these three men—father, husband, and politician. Book upon book are filled with words about their aspirations, their frustrations, their deaths. But all of that is another story—and not the story I tell to you tonight. (MEG *replaces the book on the table. The lights come up on* WILLIAM ROPER, *crouched in the downstage area; he urgently whispers:*)

WILL. Meg! *Meg!*

MEG. (*Startled, she looks about.*) Will? Where are you?

WILL. Over here. In the bushes. Come!

MEG. (*Laughing and crossing to him.*) You lunatic.

(*In a flash,* WILL *disentangles himself and lunges at* MARGARET. *He is "aflame" with passion. In a frenzy, he kisses* MEG, *embraces her, throws off a boot, tears his belt buckle undone, rips at his shirt, and tugs at her to join him.*)

WILL. Oh, Meg, oh Meg, meg, meg, meg, meg . . .

MEG. (*With growing command.*) Will. *Will.* WILL. (*He stops, red faced and imploring. She is imperious.*) The vow. First the vow, Will.

WILL. (*Groaning.*) Oh, but Meg, I l-love you. . . . (WILL *is on his knees, his face pressed in her skirts, laboring to find the breath to vow.*)

MEG. "I, William Roper" . . . (*Pats* WILL'*s head.*) Come, come, Willie— "I, William Roper" . . .

WILL. "I, William Roper" . . . I don't remember anymore.

MEG. (*Patiently.*) "Vow to be guided by my wife, Margaret More" . . .

WILL. "Vow to be guided by my wife, Margaret More"—oh, Meg, can't we—

MEG. —"in all matters civil, religious, and domestic" . . .

WILL. —"in all matters civil, religious, and domestic" . . .

MEG. "to abide by her council,"

WILL. "to abide by her council,"

MEG. "to acknowledge her supremacy,"

WILL. "to acknowledge her supremacy,"

MEG. "and complete authority in the upbringing of our offspring"

WILL. "and-complete-authority-in-the-upbringing-of-our-offspring" (*The words are rushed in his eagerness: he is very horny.*)

MEG. "for all our married life."

WILL. "for all our married life." (*Pause.*) Now, Meg, now?

MEG. (*She looks down upon his upturned moronic face, and is pensively touched.*) You really are an idiot, William—oh, but I do love you. . . . (MEG *bends, kisses his hair perfunctorily, and abruptly begins to pace, forgetting or ignoring his frustration.*)

WILL. (*Disappointed and crouched.*) Oh, Meg, oh Meg . . .

MEG. (*Stopping in thought.*) William: I may have you convert back to Catholicism again. (WILL *hastily starts to cross himself*—MEG *halts his arm.*) —but not until I tell you.

WILL. I understand, Meg: not until you tell me.

MEG. (*Bursting out, pleased with herself.*) You see, it's all a matter of strategy, Will. Oh, you wouldn't understand . . . (*With patience.*) Papa would never consent to my marrying the village idiot—so I engage myself to a Protestant—that's ten times worse than any idiot in father's eyes—and when you do convert, he'll embrace you with relief—his future son-in-law, the Catholic . . . village idiot! So stupid, but oh, so orthodox!! You see? (*But* WILL *obviously does not.* WILL *continues to gaze up at* MEG *with blank, but total devotion.*)

WILL. (*Eagerly.*) I see, Meg, I see.

MEG. (*Suddenly remembering. With reproach.*) But Will, when I told you to be Protestant, I meant you to be . . . somewhat theologically subtle.

WILL. Thea . . . subl—sus—?

MEG. —What is this I hear about the Inn last week?

WILL. The Inn? (WILL *remembers; evading* MEG's *inquiry with shame.*) I didn't mean anything. . . .

MEG. Didn't mean anything! Did you, or did you not, publicly state that the Pope "pisses in the Eucharist"?

· WILL. (*Sullenly.*) He does so p-piss in the Eucharist.

MEG. He does not.

WILL. Allright: he does not.

MEG. Oh, Will! (*To herself.*) That's not reformation, that's heresy! (*To* WILL.) You can only get away with so much before they'll burn your little Saxon body to purify your little Saxon soul—never taking into account your little Saxon mind—and then, where would I find another such congenial moron to marry me? (MEG *embraces* WILL *to soothe him.*) Hey, now Will . . . (*They kiss;* ALICE MORE *stands up stage left, and calls out.*)

ALICE. Margaret!

(MEG *and* WILL *freeze in their embrace.*)

MEG. Oh, Jesus.

ALICE. (*Shrill.*) Margaret! Where are you! Aha—there you are . . . (ALICE's *mouth pops open in dismay and disbelief.*) Who is that with you? Is that William Roper?! Stay right where you are! I'm coming out this instant—

(ALICE *goes in search of a willow switch;* WILLIAM, *who has been paralyzed with fear, suddenly becomes active.* WILL *rushes to his cast off boot, struggles with it, while pulling up his half-fallen down breeches with one hand.*)

WILL. Oh, migod, Meg. I'm off.

MEG. Don't leave, Will. (*Impishly.*) Stay with me, Lover— (MEG *starts to embrace* WILL.)

WILL. She'll horsewhip me: that's what she said. Stop it, Meg—I can't stay. She's going to—Meg, let go—I'm scared of Mrs. More—last time she said—

MEG. Be brave! I won't let her hurt you. (WILL's

back is turned to MEG; WILL *struggles to run off; her arms are locked around his waist. Full of the devil at* ALICE'S *approach,* MEG *becomes passionate and attacks* WILL.) Oh, Will, oh, Will, Will, Will. (MEG *kisses his neck, and bites into* WILL'S *jacket.*)

WILL. Meg! Meg, for the love of Christ, let go! Meg!! (*At the sight of* MRS. MORE *coming with a willow switch,* WILL *shrieks and tears loose, leaving his jacket behind.* MEG *nonchalantly faces* ALICE'S *puffed and infuriated face.*)

MEG. Ah, Spring. It's the molting season, you know.

ALICE. You're not funny. Where did that village idiot, that William Roper go? I'll beat some sense into him—

MEG. Into William Roper?

ALICE. (*Attempting to be reasonable.*) I don't know why you insist on shaming your family, Meg. You have already called public attention to yourself by reading and writing pamphlets—proclaiming your freak nature to the world—but now, now you have to diddle about with Protestants and Bedlamites! (MEG *starts to say something, but is silent.*) I will not have that drooling monkey set foot in my house! Do you hear? (*Again,* MEG *starts to say something, but is silent.*) I don't know what you can possibly see in him—

MEG. Well, to be truthful—

ALICE. —don't tell me! You have no shame. That comes from your Greek lessons . . . such brazenness! I have married into a family of maniacs. Had you been mine, you'd be learning to cook, and clean, and care for a decent, honest, intelligent husband. But I've submitted to your father, and watched him warp and twist your mind into some medical curio! But *this* I will not submit to!! Not in my family!! If William Roper so much as comes near, he'll be missing more

than common sense on his own wedding day!!! (ALICE
huffs her retreat. MEG *smiles at the audience.*)

MEG. That, dear ladies and gentlemen, was my beloved stepmother, Alice More. Ah, but I know what
you're thinking. There's more than fate that drives a
man to martyrdom, yes? Sometimes—tho' perhaps
he'll never admit it—sometimes I feel that my father
understands exactly why I shall marry Will Roper—
and envies me my domestic peace. (MEG *pauses,
fondly.*) Well, I suppose you're anxious to meet the
great Sir Thomas More? My father. Some standard
words of caution before I introduce you to him—
Great men never look like great men—at least, not in
the beginning; they only transform into those heroic
busts and monuments near the end. So be gentle in
your first impressions—he's very great, and very dear,
and . . . slightly ridiculous.

(*Lights up on* SIR THOMAS MORE, *seated at the table
at center, vigorously scratching away in the book,
and at his legs. He is slight of stature, scrawny
in build, with thin pathetic legs in stockings which
bag—and a look of mild embarrassment on his
face. Rather shabbily dressed, his clothes usually
sport the crumbs from his last meal.* MEG *tiptoes
to the area behind him, unseen and quiet, so as
not to disturb him. He immediately puts down
his pen and smiles, without turning.*)

MORE. Good morning, Meg.
MEG. (*Throwing her arms around his shoulders and
kissing him extravagantly.*) Good morning, Papa!
MORE. (*Looking amused.*) No, now don't tell me.
Let me guess. William Roper's been here this morning.
MEG. (*Grinning.*) How ever did you guess?

MORE. Your mother's been fussing her confidences to the chickens; all my morning eggs were addled. (*They smile warmly at one another.*)

MEG. Well, it's better to have her fussing at the chickens. . . .

MORE. Well, well. It's only her way, Meg—she's concerned. We're all concerned. She doesn't want an i— (MORE *does not finish the "diot."*) . . . a man of dubious intellect for a son, and I don't wish to have a Protestant for a son-in-law.

MEG. Is that your sole objection, Papa?

MORE. (*Evasively.*) I have every faith in your ability to pick and choose for yourself among suitors.

MEG. (*Firmly.*) There have been none.

MORE. Well, well. (*Awkward silence.*) I'm sure you have your reasons for selecting Will. . . . (MORE *trails off; then brightly.*) And I'm sure he has sterling qualities. . . .

MEG. Papa . . .

MORE. Yes?

MEG. Kindly name one.

MORE. One?

MEG. One sterling quality of Will's that you've noticed during our furtive courtship behind the chicken barn.

MORE. Oh. Uhm . . . he has such a nice, vacant smile.

MEG. (*Refusing to let* MORE *evade her.*) Papa, you know why I'll marry Will,.don't you?

MORE. (*Gently.*) I know I want to be grandfather to your children, no matter what the reasons.

MEG. (*Raptly.*) Yes, children! We'll make an entire army of scholars, marching against the dark, just ripe for our indoctrination—

MORE. —Well, before that happens, I ask you to

observe the rituals of marriage. I'm a believer in forms, Meg. I do not ask you or your husband to share my convictions; but do observe my conventions. (*Rhetorically.*) Within the politically tense atmosphere in which we live, it is folly to be non-conformist, whether in appearance or opinion. No man's heart will be examined as long as he mumbles his pater noster.

MEG. And if Will should come back to the fold?

MORE. (*With difficulty.*) I will embrace him as one of the family. But until then, I must invoke a paternal veto against this marriage never before used. Meg, I cannot turn you out into a hostile world without protection. It is foolhardy to marry a dissenter. All the security I have tried to build—

MEG. —Papa, I know. (MEG *slips her arms around* MORE.) I won't displease you in this one thing. Until Will converts, confesses and communes again with Mother Church, I'll not marry. But what is this nonsense of my being "turned out into a hostile world"?

MORE. Well, I meant—

MEG. —Married or not, here I'll remain with you. Isn't that what we've planned? How would you write without me? Or run the school? (MEG *spies crumbs on the front of his clothes.*) Who would brush the crumbs from your clothes, for that matter? (MEG *laughs and brushes* MORE *clean with a critical eye.*) There. William Roper will make no difference to our relationship, Papa. I'd give the world up first. As it is, I'll be the happiest of all women— (*To the audience.*) On the one hand, I'll have intercourse with Will, and on the other hand, I'll hold intercourse with my father. (*To* MORE.) My life will be neatly compartmentalized, eh, Papa?

MORE. (*Placated, he has turned out the last.*) What, my dear? Yes, yes, I dare say. Let's have no more of this now, Meg; we'll discuss it later . . . (*Embarrassed and pleased,* MORE *sits back down and picks up his pen.* MEG *is left to her own revery.* MORE *scribbles a bit, but watches* MEG *critically from the corner of his eye. Then with a meek air, knowing that* MEG *will soon be displeased:*) Oh, by the way, Meg. I expect I'll be leaving home for a few days soon. I'll want you to take care of the school—

MEG. (*Alarmed.*) Leaving? Why?

MORE. It's an instinct I have for trouble. I expect the King will call a council shortly, and I shall be wanted . . . for how long, heaven knows.

MEG. Have you received word?

MORE. No—but Cromwell's coming; I can sniff him a mile away. The smell of political aspiration is heavy on the air. Take my word for it; Henry, like a spoiled child, won't take no for an answer from the Pope. He'll have his Anne, even if all the Cardinal Woolsey's must first go hang. I don't wish to become involved. . . . I have enough difficulty with my own marital affairs than to presume to advise. . . .

MEG. Then why do you become involved? Can't you resign from the King's council for reasons of health? It's nothing but interference with our life here! And it's becoming more frequent, Papa, really it is. . . .

MORE. (*Sighing poetically.*) If only I could stay here and talk with you. . . .

MEG. You can! What do you care for politics? Your great Utopian mind is wasted on such . . . trivia! You've called it that yourself, Papa. And haven't you told me a man's first duty is to his family? Before his "civic responsibilities"? Why, that's revolutionary, Papa! It takes greatness and nobility to renounce the world and to fashion utopia from one's family . . . (*Here* MEG *can't resist a joke.*) —Besides, no man before you has dare—with pen quill in hand—to face the "great hooked beak of the harpy"!

MORE. Meg! (MORE *is slightly shocked.*) That is no way to talk about . . . (MORE *hides a smile with difficulty, turning a laugh into a cough.*) your mother.

MEG. They're Erasmus' words, dear father, not mine. I often think you run to London only to escape her—oh, don't protest, I know all you're going to say: how she loves me as her own, how she takes care of me, how grateful we should both be. . . . (*Exasperated.*) Well, that may well be true, but you can't take me with you to your councils! Papa, I have no one to talk to. And who will teach me Latin while you are gone?

MORE. That tactic won't work; you don't need my help any longer, it's no use pretending. You're teaching your tutor now. I've sent your letters to Erasmus before, and he couldn't tell the difference between your style and mine—except for a slight superiority in your letters. (MORE *is obviously very proud.*) As a matter of fact, while I'm gone, I'd like you to take over writing the family history which I promised to complete for him—

MEG. (*Delighted.*) The family history! (MEG *eagerly rushes to the table.*) Could I? How far have you come?

MORE. (*With mischief.*) Let's see,—we're up to ancient times now. . . . (MORE *snatches the quill, and scribbles while* MEG *reads over his shoulder.*)

MEG. "The dominant force in the More household, around which the house revolved, was Mistress Margaret More, age eight and ten, a "petulans muliercula"— (*translating.*) a . . . saucy snippet! Ah, but Papa! You are leaving out the most important part— (MEG *giggles and pushes* MORE *back; seizing the pen,* MEG *writes while her father reads over her shoulder.*)

MORE. "This saucy snippet was the result of the erudite training of the saintly Sir More, a curious "valgus vir doctus fama" . . . (*Translating.*) bow-legged scholar of renown. . . . (*They both laugh,* MEG *merrily, and* MORE *a bit ruefully . . . then he asks, self-consciously.*) Am I really . . . ah, bow-legged? (MORE *is anxious to appear casual, but waits for re-assurance.*)

MEG. Papa, it's your most endearing trait, I assure you. (MORE *is crestfallen;* MEG *smiles fondly.*) When I see those poor orphan legs of yours, I smile and laugh and cry inside, all at once. . . . (MORE *has walked away behind her, and tries to glance back-wards at the back of his legs;* MEG *turns and catches* MORE *in his contortion—and realizes she has struck his ego.* MORE *flushes,* MEG *quickly changes the subject.*) Why are you writing our family history for Erasmus?

MORE. It all came about as an extension of our dis-cussion of words—words which in the attempt to cap-ture truth inevitably become fabrications—and partic-ularly offensive as history. So rather than having others fabricate our lives, we shall do it ourselves.

MEG. Do you think we will be so important that others would want to write about us?

MORE. (*Insincerely.*) Perhaps not. Actually, the real reason for writing family histories is for the flattery and nostalgia of one's family.

MEG. Ah, no, father—I am not to be so easily fooled. Somewhere in that gentle head of yours there have been dangerous dreams lurking—dreams of political success and fame; have there not? (*Sadly.*) You must want to go to London very badly.

MORE. I never want to leave you, Meg. I don't think my life can be better spent than here, talking and

writing with you. Your education will always be my
proudest accomplishment. Sometimes I feel . . . no,
you'll laugh at me—

MEG. I won't laugh at you.

MORE. I often feel maternal about you. (MORE *is
shy, and glances at* MEG.) Do you understand? (*Moved
and mute,* MEG *nods her head.*) You have made me
much more than a father; and I feel strong because I
feel gentle. It's easy to be gentle with you. But often
I think that it's not enough to be gentle with you alone;
it's a gift that should be shared with others outside
the family—others, in the world of men, that should
be treated as family, too. (MEG's *back is turned;*
MORE *cannot see her face.*) Am I being ridiculous?

MEG. (*Turning quickly and coming to him.*) No,
Papa, no—not ridiculous to me. But—forgive me—
terribly, terribly naive. (MEG *ruffles* MORE's *hair.*) It
makes me feel maternal toward you.

(ALICE MORE, *the personification of the "hooked beak
of the harpy," has crept up behind them, and
watches* MEG *ruffle her husband's hair.*)

ALICE. Husband. (MORE *and* MEG *start.*) Master
Cromwell has arrived and waits outside. If you ask
me, he acts more like a fishmonger's apprentice dressed
in his master's suit—than a messenger from the King!
Ha! (MORE *exchanges an "I told you so" glance with*
MEG.)

MORE. He may indeed act like a fishmonger, but I
assure you Master Cromwell will be a political power
to reckon with—so be gentle. I hope you have been
polite?

ALICE. (*Ignoring the plea.*) . . . that may well be.
I will tell him to come in immediately—but mind you,
Thomas, he will not be staying to lunch.

MORE. Yes, love. I know I can count on your hospitable grace to company. . . . (*This last is said because* ALICE *is already out of earshot.*)

MEG. Cromwell— Well! (*Admiringly.*) You are a prophet.

MORE. (*Mock-modestly and grinning.*) It's nothing.

MEG. I always wanted to meet him. What an absurd little man he must be!

(CROMWELL, *the absurd little man, has entered and stands on the platform above. He watches and overhears the following:*)

MORE. (*Cautiously.*) Watch him well, Meg. He's climbing so fast your nose will bleed watching his ascent.

MEG. Surely you don't like him?

MORE. (*Hastily.*) No—but I must admire his mind —he's certainly acute. (*Jumps.*) I'd better go meet him. Your mother may be . . . entertaining him. (MORE *scurries to meet* CROMWELL, *and is startled to see him.*) Oh. (*Then heartily:*) Welcome, Master Cromwell!

CROMWELL. I received your message, Sir Thomas (MORE *motions him to speak softly.*) and came as immediately as I received necessary notification for the council's meeting. I hope I'm not too tardy?

MORE. Not at all. You are very prompt and courteous. (*Low.*) I'm sure you must be aware that I need a business excuse to go to London; it was kind indeed of His Majesty to furnish one.

CROMWELL. (*Discreetly.*) I understand. (*They smile, and approach the area where* MEG *patiently waits.*)

MORE. Master Cromwell, this is my daughter Meg. (MEG *smiles coldly while* CROMWELL *bows.*)

CROMWELL. (*Gallantly and pompously.*) I am pleasantly surprised to find your beauty surpasses reports of your intelligence. . . .

MEG. (*Not pleased, colder still.*) Thank you, sir. I, too, am surprised to find your intelligence surpasses reports of your beauty. . . . (CROMWELL's *face blankly stares,* MORE *is aghast.*)

MORE. Meg! I'm sure, that, um, my daughter means—

MEG. —Oh, Master Cromwell will understand and forgive. I can never pass an opportunity for quipping; it is nothing at all personal.

CROMWELL. (*Blandly smiling.*) I assure you I am flattered by the ready intimacy with which you tease me, Mistress More.

MEG. You are kind—isn't he kind, father? (MORE *nervously paces behind* MEG; *getting no response,* MEG *turns to* CROMWELL.) Do you know, Master Cromwell, that father intuitively knew of your coming here? Not but ten minutes ago, he foretold it to me— (MORE *behind her back, pantomimes urgently to* CROMWELL *to play along.*) Is not that amazing?

CROMWELL. Ah, Miss More, that intuition is the secret of a successful politician—

MEG. My father is not a politician.

CROMWELL. Indeed, he has a politician's instinct combined with a nobleman's integrity—which makes him a statesman. . . .

MORE. (*Trying to hide his pleasure.*) We scholars can never match the consummate skill in words of one well-read in a king's looks. But come, we waste your time, sir.

CROMWELL. Very well, then, sir. To business. (CROMWELL *bows to* MEG *and waits.*)

MORE. (*After waiting for* CROMWELL *to continue.*) Well, sir, what is the business at hand? (*A pause again.*)

CROMWELL. (*Who has been waiting for* MEG *to leave.*) —Uh, I beg your pardon, Sir Thomas. I did not wish to show disrespect to the young lady by discussing such mundane matters of state in front of her.

MORE. (*While* MEG *smiles to herself ironically.*) Pray continue, Master Cromwell. Meg is my book-keeper, theologian, daughter-confessor, and council member in one. There is nothing I feel competent to act upon without her advice. (*To* MEG.) Without you, I think I'd do no more business at all— (*Smiles.*) "no mundane matters of state"— (*To* CROMWELL.) So please, let us all continue.

CROMWELL. (*With a look of repressed disapproval, he rummages under his cloak for various papers.*) Very good, sir.

MORE. I gather such notions about daughters discomfort you, Master Cromwell?

CROMWELL. (*Glibly.*) Not at all, Sir Thomas. It takes a remarkable man to raise a remarkable daughter. . . .

MORE. Aha, Meg—you see the epitome of modern day diplomacy in action before you.

MEG. (*Bemused.*) I do indeed, father.

(MORE *moves to the table and sits;* MEG *stands to his left, while* CROMWELL *presents the papers to* MORE'S *right—as he lays the papers on the table,* MEG *curiously presses closer—and exchanges a rapid glance with* CROMWELL.)

CROMWELL. Tomorrow's meeting is primarily a discussion of strategy for the petition to His Holiness to annul Henry's union with Queen Catherine. All of this has been previously considered. Cardinal Woolsey has drafted a preliminary paper—here is a copy—listing all the causes and facts for Henry's annulment to the Queen; the prior committment between Catherine and his deceased brother Arthur; the need for a male heir to the throne—nothing particularly new here; but kindly glance through the paper and make suggestions freely. The Cardinal— (*Confidently.*) and I might say, the King himself—hold your opinion in esteem.

MORE. How much time is allotted for ratification of the petition by the Council?

CROMWELL. His Majesty is impatient. (CROMWELL *winks to* MORE.) So is Mistress Boleyn. . . . (CROMWELL *sniggers; his joke falling short,* CROMWELL *clears his throat.*) Within the week. . . .

MORE. Within the week!

MEG. (*Quickly.*) I can easily run the school, Papa.

MORE. Yes, thank you, my dear. Well, we shall soon see if your speculation is accurate—

CROMWELL. —speculation, Sir Thomas?

MORE. My daughter wages that the Pope will refuse annulment due to the difficulties in both Spanish and French relations with Rome—

CROMWELL. That's very interesting, I'm sure. The abstractions of academicians are always interesting to consider. But I can assure that the whole petition is a mere formality, with the dispensation already granted. Such is the prediction of Lord Chancellor Woolsey, at any rate.

MEG. (*To* MORE.) But the question is being examined only in isolation—which is political fallacy. . . .

CROMWELL. (*Pompously.*) It is a pity that the Council can not hear your "speculations" directly, Mistress More; they are very illuminating, I'm sure. . . .

MORE. Oh, they'll hear her speculations indirectly as long as I'm a member of the Council. Will any other matters be discussed?

CROMWELL. No; I think that sums it up neatly, Sir Thomas. We await you at Whitehall early in the morning for your good counsel. Farewell, sir.

MORE. I hear that there's a report circulating that my wife's culinary skill surpasses Meg's intelligence. May I counsel you to stay to dine with us?

CROMWELL. (*He hesitates, and then:*) I should be delighted to stay and dine—

MEG. (*Coldly polite.*) We should all be delighted by your company, Master Cromwell. . . . (*They look at one another.*)

CROMWELL. You will both pardon me for refusing your kind invitation, I hope. I have the king's business to attend to.

MORE. Yes, of course. Good day, sir.

CROMWELL. (*Bowing.*) Sir Thomas. Mistress More. (MEG *silently inclines her head.* CROMWELL *quickly leaves.*)

MEG. What an odious little man! With such men in the state, it is no wonder you prefer to stay here with us. Don't you father?

MORE. You know I do. I must confess I feel peculiar in the first place being on the Council, and passing judgement on such a matter as this. No man can or should legislate on a man's relation to his wife, king or no. It's a private matter, and I don't feel presumptuous enough to advise the king at all . . . though of course, Henry doesn't want advice, but rather assent.

I'll give him what he wants, nod my head, and return here quickly to Chelsea.

MEG. This will be your last year on the Council, Papa? Won't it be?

MORE. If I can resign gracefully, I will.

MEG. Good. There is no way you can serve Henry and me at the same time. I'm afraid Master Cromwell did not appreciate my "speculations" . . .

MORE. Particularly when you may very well be right.

MEG. Good! I will sabotage all your political "friendships" with such men as he; you must bring all your acquaintances to meet me once; and then I will never have to part with you again. An end to these weeks on the king's business! Then we can finish our writing together, Papa, without interference.

MORE. (*Bemused.*) Just think, Meg—no doubt if you were Cromwell's daughter, right this moment you'd be squinting your eyes over some piece of plain sewing by the fire—pricking your finger on the needle each time your mind wanders to that handsome inn-keeper's son, and superstitiously tossing salt over your shoulder. How would you like that? Buzzing with the charmaids, and praying to St. Anne? (*Pause.*) Though I wonder to what extent my blind lunacy has harmed you. Perhaps you would be a happier woman, eh?

MEG. (*Holding* MORE *briefly.*) Oh, Papa—I'm not unhappy now. A bit lonely from time to time—especially when you occupy yourself away from home with such trivia as popes and kings and matters of state! But surely it's worth all the charmaid's gossip in the world to share Plato with you. . . . I do wonder, tho', Papa—if my brother John had been born the eldest, would you not have nurtured his mind at my expense?

MORE. John has not your wit. And have not your

sisters already received an education which makes the townspeople gawk at them in the streets? But it's true, you have a gift far beyond plain sewing and embroidery—that typical ignorance that passes for "breeding" among English gentlewomen. . . .

MEG. I'm not denying that I'm different from the others. But even so, why did you give me so much? Why did you decide to teach me Latin and Greek? I'm not complaining, because I'm ever so grateful to you— if you've separated me from kin and kind, you have also opened up an entire world of solace past my sisters' fantasies. It's rather thrilling, Papa. I sometimes stay transfixed over a page in a book, and the words lose meaning. Because I think—I am very likely the only woman in the world right now poring over these words—there is no other woman. I am unique. It's uncharted territory that together, you and I, are exploring. But Papa, does that make me a freak of nature?

MORE. No, not a freak—a mystery unraveling. When I first married your mother—I was so young and awed by women, then, and though several years older than Jane, and a rising barrister—still, I stopped mute in the face of her mystery. I, Thomas More, marry a woman! Become a familiar with this alien force, and live from day to day never penetrating the distance between man and woman! You may well smile at my naivete. (*The repressed laugh within* MEG *breaks forth, and* MORE *smiles sheepishly.*) Yes, well—I am still awed. Men live their lives out never realizing that there are dark continents waiting to be discovered, whole new worlds of experience—a foot away from them, in the minds of their wives. What, I wondered, does she think, this Jane Colt, when she stares into the fire? Where does her soul retreat at night, when her rib cage rises and falls beside me? So I determined to uncover the secret of your sex. But your mother—she was sparkling, by God, and as awed by Greek as I by her—

MEG. —never revealed the mystery.

MORE. Exactly. She died first before I discovered her.

MEG. Poor Papa.

MORE. Ah, but God sent me a consolation. I turned around the day of her funeral, and caught sight of you—a mere moppet of ten still, Meg—with clumsy chubby legs and stringy hair that refused the rationality of comb and water—and I saw it.

MEG. You saw . . . ?

MORE. In your eyes. I saw the Eve-laughter peeping out of your eyes, taunting me with the mystery again.

MEG. But I was a child!

MORE. You were born wise— (*Sighing.*) you were born female. And so the great experiment and devotion of my life began.

MEG. (*To herself.*) —the "medical curio"—

MORE. What?

MEG. Well, Papa? Are you on the right track? Are you uncovering the mystery of woman?

MORE. (*Smiling down at her.*) —It's too early to tell. I need another forty years or so. . . .

MEG. (*To herself.*) An experiment. . . . (*Smiling sadly, and then not smiling at all,* MEG *paces away from* MORE.)

MORE. Is something wrong, pet?

MEG. (*Shrugging.*) I'm not sure. It's nothing, I suppose. I just suddenly feel totally alone.

MORE. Because of something I—?

(*We hear and see* ALICE MORE *huffing across the stage,
with a limp and stunned* WILL ROPER *dangling
from her grip. As she talks,* WILL *babbles.*)

ALICE. Now we'll just see, Master Roper, the result
of your defiance! We'll just see! You've pushed me
once too often! Chicken-barn loitering! You were
warned this very morning! Once too often! Well,
we'll just see . . .

WILL. (*In shock.*) Na-na-na-na-na-na-na-na-na

(ALICE *deposits* WILL *on the floor in front of* MORE;
WILL *becomes a puddle on the floor.* MEG *struggles
to keep a straight face.*)

ALICE. Husband. I demand retribution. I won't have
my authority flouted by this village snipe! This va-
cancy! He's been warned and now he's deliberately
defied me! Defied me!! Either you immediately stand
up and support me, or—or— Either Will Roper goes—
or you can prepare your own meals around here! I
mean what I say!

MORE. Now, Angel, don't be angry. I'll try to. . . .

ALICE. He's never going to show his face here again!
If horsewhipping was good enough for my father, it's
good enough for. . . . (ALICE *stops to realize what she
has said;* MEG *sputters.*)

MORE. Meg! This is a grave business!

MEG. I know it is. I'm sorry. (*Kneeling to the puddle
on the floor; gently:*) Uh, Will. I don't know quite
how to put this. . . . Is . . . um . . . anything . . .
"missing"?

ALICE. No more than he was born without.

MEG. (*Relieved.*) Oh. That's all right, then.

MORE. I want tó talk with Will alone.

WILL. (*Softly.*) Na-na-na-na-na

MEG. —Shhh! It's okay, Will. No one will hurt you.

ALICE. Husband! A horsewhipping!

MORE. (*Standing impressively erect and flaring.*) Wife! I will take care of this! (MORE *withstands* ALICE'S *glare;* ALICE *leaves indignantly. The three of them immediately exhale and relax. Pause. Then* MORE, *timidly:*) Meg? I really should speak to Will alone.

MEG. I know, father. But please, may we first exchange a few words privately? (MORE *nods and walks upstage.*) All right, now, William, everything will be just fine. Father will help us. How do you feel?

WILL. (*He feels himself.*) A-a-ll right. (*He is still shaken.*)

MEG. Good. How do you feel spiritually?

WILL. (*Starts to feel himself; then vacantly:*) Huh?

MEG. Oh, Will—don't you feel different? Changed? Are you not burning with the glow inside? A fervor and fear shaking your frame? (WILL *stares at her.*) Listen! Do you not hear? (WILL *strains to listen.*) Will! The celestial voices! (WILL *still listens . . .* MEG *regards his upturned gullible face with disdainful amusement.*)

WILL. (*Eagerly.*) I don't hear anything, Meg. I'm-m trying.

MEG. Never mind, Will. Allow me to translate: the voices are calling you back to Mother Church. It's Conversion-time. When father comes back, you're to tell him that you've had a change of heart—you've heard the voices, seen the light, etc.

WILL. (*Dawning.*) Oh, I see, Meg. (WILL *starts to cross himself.*)

MEG. That's right. Whatever father asks, just say "Yes, sir." Understand?

WILL. "Yes, sir."

MEG. That's my love. (MEG *kisses* WILL.) Tomorrow we'll have the banns read out in the parish church. . . .

WILL. Meg—

MEG. What's the matter, Will?

WILL. Are you sure you wanta marry me? You c'n change your mind now, if you wanta.

MEG. That's very sweet, Will. I love you.

WILL. 'Cause marriage is forever.

MEG. Not if King Henry gets his way, and the Council supports his petition for divorce: Who knows? Kings set the trend; it might become fashionable—

WILL. (*Aghast.*) Meg! Your father would never permit it!!

MEG. Permit?? Permit what?

WILL. The King's divorce—breaking holy wedlock! "Whom God hath t-tied together—"

MEG. —My God, Will! You sound Catholic already!! Besides, my father doesn't split theological hairs—he's told me so. This is politics, not ethics. You wouldn't understand. Father observes the forms of religion; but underneath he's a free-thinker. He doesn't presume to judge the faith of others—we must "observe his conventions, not his convictions." He's a very subtle man, Will. Perhaps you'll get to understand him better in time.

WILL. Your father's not a f-free-thinker. He's a deeply religious man.

MEG. How would you know?

WILL. 'Cause it takes a religious man to have a—a —non-believer for a daughter.

MEG. (*She is stopped.*) Heavens. "From out the

mouths of morons—" Do you know what, Will? There's a very thin line in you separating idiocy from profundity. . . . Well, anyway, let us observe the conventions. We have the rest of our lives to discuss conviction. Now, then, when father comes back, you're to say, "Sir Thomas, I have seen the light. I wish to convert." Okay? (WILL *starts to mouth the words to memorize*—"Sir-Thomas-I-Have . . .) My father will take it from there. (*Calling* MORE.) Father . . . (MORE *comes downstage*.) There's something Will wishes to tell you— (MEG *nudges* WILL.) Will?

WILL. "S-s-sir Thomas . . . I-have-seen-the-light. I-wish-to-convert." (*Looking at* MEG.) Is that right? (MORE *regards them both suspiciously*.)

MORE. I think you had better leave Will and I alone for a bit, Meg. Please wait outside.

MEG. (*She leaves, and faces the audience:*) And I waited outside— (MEG *smiles*.) But I listened.

MORE. So, um, Will—you wish to convert, is that it?

WILL. (*Stupidly*.) "Yes, sir."

MORE. You realize the errors of your ways?

WILL. Yes, sir.

MORE. That only the one and universal Church can redeem man from eternal torment? That the Pope is the true representative of Peter and Paul? That the wine and the bread transubstantiate into the blood and body of Christ who died to save our sins? Do you understand all this, Will?

WILL. (*Faltering*.) "Yes, sir."

MORE. (*Skeptically*.) Well, that's fine, Will. Perhaps one of these days you'll explain it all to me.

WILL. Yes, sir.

MORE. Do you convert of your own free will?

WILL. Yes, sir.

MORE. Hmmm— Have you been persuaded and coerced by alien forces away from and back to the one universal church?

WILL. Yes, sir.

MORE. I thought so. (MORE *sighs, and calls* MEG.) Meg! (MEG *walks to* WILL *and takes his arm.*) Will and I have set things straight. It seems he is once again a sheep among many on the path to salvation.

MEG. Now all that remains to be done—he has not yet asked your permission to marry me. . . . (*Both men turn in alarm to* MEG.)

MORE. Meg—!

MEG. Father—better a Catholic than a Protestant. . . . (*Imperturbable.*) Will—kneel and ask father for permission to marry me—

WILL. (*Carefully kneeling.*) —Is this right? S-sir Thomas, may I have your permission to marry your daughter?

MORE. (*Sighing.*) That's the most intelligent thing he's said all day. (*With resignation.*) My children, let us pray together, and receive your father's benediction. (MEG *and* WILL *bow heads.*) Oh, Father in Heaven, bless these children in the days of their marriage; make them fruitful and happy, and obedient to the Christian way of life. And strengthen thy servant Will Roper (MORE'S *voice rises in sarcasm.*) to avoid the temptation of heresy. Thank you, O Lord, for his conversion; keep his heart true and faithful. In the name of the Father, and the Son, and the Holy Ghost. (MEG *and* MORE *automatically cross themselves;* WILL *hesitates:*)

WILL. Now, Meg?

MEG. Now, Will. (WILL *crosses himself. Unable to control her frivolity any longer,* MEG *bursts with.*)

God be praised!! (MORE *casts an admonishing look at her sacriligious attitude—*MEG *quickly lowers her head and attempts to look innocent and pious. She does not quite succeed as the light lowers.*)

END OF ACT ONE

MEG

EG. I thought I'd wait until the ceremony was

LICE. There go my hopes of an annulment—but, you've married an annulment, haven't you?

ORE. Now, mother, please. . . .

LICE. I shall see to the refreshments; we could all some wine— (ALICE exits.)

EG. Poor woman—she's taking it rather hard.

ORE. She'll be fine in time.

EG. And you father? Do you understand? Can you give me?

ORE. There's nothing to forgive. How can I be gry at the gift of a grandchild? Even if it is from h an unlikely source . . . but I must confess, I am aken.

EG. There's no need to be. Leave all the arrange-ents to me. We can convert the study next to the assroom into a nursery, don't you think? So that I n check in on the baby in between teaching the hool.

ORE. But don't you want to nurse the child your—

EG. —Oh, no, there's no need. However could I ookkeep, write, teach and nurse? No, that's all settled, Papa— Doesn't our cook have a sister in the village?

ORE. You mean, um—Bertha? Or is it Mary?

EG. Whichever—you know the sister—the one who's always seen with a passel of runny-nosed babes about her—heaven, she's fertile. I believe she subsists on alms the year round. I thought I'd do the town council a favor and employ her as wet-nurse. After all, she has only one child yet unweaned, and she does have two breasts.

ORE. I see all is thought out.

EG. Oh, yes, we'll manage nicely. The only thing I haven't planned out is the child's sex. I don't sup-

---

ACT TWO

The set is unchanged from Act One. Music opens the act: bright as only Renaissance wedding music can be, yet tinged with an awareness of mortality. Downstage center, with his back to us, is a robed and hooded friar. WILL, perspiring in his Sunday best, and MEG, defiantly happy, enter and kneel before the friar, facing us. They cross themselves. WILL watches MEG closely, following her actions a beat late. Then:

Enter SIR THOMAS. He pauses, waits, gestures for ALICE to join him. He exits again, then re-enters with a barely civil ALICE. Angry and crying, ALICE darts fierce looks at the priest, MORE, WILL and MEG. Feeling ALICE's presence, WILL withers visibly, and is braced by MEG. We hear the priest's droning; from this tableaux, MEG rises, and hurries downstage to tell us.

MEG. William Roper and I became husband and wife in London, far from our village chapel and family priest in Chelsea. In a vast stern cathedral we stood dwarfed, side by side. We shared our insignificance at an altar consecrated by state funerals and—for a mo-ment—we were equal. (MEG *returns just in time to be in place.*)

PRIEST. And do you, Margaret More, vow to take William Roper as your husband in the name of Christ, to cherish and to hold, in sickness and in health, for

33

better and for worse, for as long as you both shall live?

MEG. I do.

PRIEST. And do you, William Roper, vow to take Margaret More as your wife in the name of Christ, to cherish and to hold, in sickness and in health, for better and for worse, for as long as you both shall live?

WILL. . . . I . . . I, uh, um, d-d-do. (WILL *glances at* MRS. MORE *and waits for the lightning to strike.* MEG *shrugs helplessly at the priest, who has paused, shaking his head.*)

PRIEST. (*With a sigh.*) Then by the power invested in me by the one, holy Apostolic Church of Rome, I now pronounce thee Man and Wife, united in Christ Our Lord. Dominus Vobiscum, et cum spirituo tuo. In nomine patri, filii et spiritus sancti, amen. (*The* PRIEST *crosses himself, all belatedly follow.* WILL *laughs with relief.*) Master Roper, you may kiss your bride. (*As* WILL *does so, the* PRIEST *crosses to* MORE *and* ALICE. *Shaking hands with* MORE:) My warmest best wishes, Sir Thomas.

MORE. Thank you, father. (MORE *eagerly goes to* MEG.)

PRIEST. (*Low, to* ALICE.) My heartfelt condolences. . . . (*As he exits, the* PRIEST *unhoods himself, flashing a familiar owl-like smile at the audience—in a split second, we recognize the actor who plays* CROMWELL— *then he is gone.*)

MORE. Son Roper— (*They shake hands.*) Ah—but daughter— (MEG *and* MORE *embrace, laughing and clinging.*) Do you know, Meg—today makes me sure that I made the right decision so many years ago. . . .

MEG. Which decision is that, Father?

MORE. My decision not to take the vows of priesthood. Did you not know? Before I met your mother. . . . (*Wistfully.*) Oh, the temptation of blissful silence,

of contemplation, of chastity— have missed this exquisitely pa

MEG. You'll always remain r fessor, Papa. . . .

(*They both become aware of a* WILL, *shrinking behind the* ALICE, *stiff, who with effort*

ALICE. I—I wish you joy, Meg.

MEG. (*Surprised.*) Thank you, M a moment; MEG *pecks her cheek.*)

MORE. (*Mildly.*) And now, my will be kin and kind to one anot (ALICE *closes her eyes with a look*

WILL. I will try to be a good More—

MORE. There! For love of me, friends— (MEG *and* MORE *nudge the* resolutely *presents her cheek to kiss.* tiptoes *to kiss—suddenly.*)

WILL. Oahhhh—excuse me— (*Stric* he rushes off.)

MORE. Is he not well? It must be my dear. . . .

MEG. Don't be alarmed; nor offende As a matter of fact, Will's perfectly filling our contract.

MORE. Contract?

MEG. I agreed to have the child if h the morning sickness.

MORE. The child!

ALICE. I knew it. Innocent bundling bel indeed!

pose it matters, tho'. Whether boy or girl, I'm sure it will take after its noble grandsire.

MORE. If it's a boy, I bequeath him my books—but if it's a girl. . . .

MEG. Along with the family books, you'd best bequeath her an amply noble dowry to match.

MORE. Yes, I dare say. Margaret, not to be unduly pessimistic—but, um, what happens should the child—"take after" its father?

MEG. I've already thought of that. We dedicate the child to the monastery or a nunnery.

MORE. Meg! May I remind you where—

MEG. Oh, come, Father—this country is running amuck with half-crazed nuns and monks. Who notices? As long as they're devout—

MORE. Please, Meg, do try to be more delicate in consideration of my position. And here you are still warm with the sacrament of marriage upon you.

MEG. Papa, I'm sorry. You know I mean no harm; we happen to think the same, but we feel differently. Heavens! You've become so solemn of late! If you had taken the vow of priesthood, you'd be a jollier, more carefree man today. Right now our priest is superfluously drinking my health, downing his tenth bumper of wine—and oggling at the serving maids.

MORE. Well—all men have their frailties; I apologize for mine. I've been preoccupied of late— I'm sure in time this political furor will die down and we'll be left to translate Latin again in Chelsea. Will you excuse me if I plead guilty of solemnity due to matters of state?

MEG. (*Lightly.*) I'll not forgive your mind for meditating today, Papa. You promised me your undivided attention; and I hold you to it. Didn't we arrange the wedding here in London to give you a day's holi-

day? I'm sure King Henry's not worrying about his
marital affairs right this moment—why should you?
Let Anne Boleyn entertain him; I'll entertain you.

MORE. I've almost forgotten how to relax. But I'll
try.

(CROMWELL *enters.*)

MEG. (*Low.*) Oh, God. I smell a Cromwell coming.

CROMWELL. Sir Thomas, Mistress Roper: May I
pay my respects to the bride? (CROMWELL *bows.*)

MEG. Ah, Master Cromwell. How kind of you to
attend. It comes as a . . . surprise.

CROMWELL. I must admit that I am here on the
instructions of the council, however much I would like
to toast healths. You must pardon the intrusion of
business; as Mistress Boleyn said to the King, "Business before pleasure,"— (CROMWELL *has held out his
hand as a whore holds hers out for payment; at his
own joke, he sniggers coarsely;* MORE'S *mouth twitches
as he tries to suppress a smile.* MEG *is not amused.*
CROMWELL *controls himself.*) Sir Thomas is required
to come with me immediately.

MEG. I'm afraid that's impossible! Now? It's out of
the question, Papa—isn't it?

CROMWELL. I'm afraid the wheels of state turn even
as one's life may stand still.

MEG. (*Drily.*) What a dizzy perspective you must
have, then, on affairs of state—you never stop spinning.

MORE. Excuse me, Meg— (*Drawing* CROMWELL
aside.) Is it absolutely necessary that I leave immediately? I've—

CROMWELL. The Papal legate has arrived unex-
pectedly early—

MORE. Here! Today! In London? When?

CROMWELL. A few hours ago—Woolsey is detaining him with hospitality; but His Eminence seems eager to convene a meeting first thing tomorrow morning.

MORE. Does the King know?

CROMWELL. His Majesty expresses confidence in your capabilities.

MORE. But Cardinal Woolsey—

CROMWELL. —is "indisposed." The King wishes you to organize the arguments.

MORE. I see. I will organize the evidence, but I can not be expected to voice the opinions—I have told His Majesty my mind on this.

CROMWELL. His Majesty does not wish you to violate your mind. Just see to the legal details. You are a lawyer of brilliance beneath your scruples, Sir. The King wishes you to see to details, facts, and organization. "Chancellor" Woolsey will use these as he sees fit.

MORE. I see.

MEG. (*Coming up to them.*) May I not know what has happened?

CROMWELL. Mistress Roper—

MORE. —It's highly confidential, dear—

MEG. I have yet to betray a trust. Cardinal Campeggio has come from Rome unannounced, is that not right?

CROMWELL. (*Startled.*) How did you—

MEG. My father has taught me how to add one plus one. I will remain quiet.

MORE. Yes, we need time to prepare. (*To* CROMWELL.) I will take my leave and join you soon.

CROMWELL. (*To* MEG.) Sometime in the future, Mistress Roper, I would like to chat with you about spinning wheels of state.

MEG. It would be a pleasure. (CROMWELL *takes his leave. There is a pause.*) It can't be helped, Papa. I understand.

MORE. I'm sorry. It will be over all the sooner; in a few weeks I can come home. And now I have a favor to ask you.

MEG. You know that whatever you ask it is my pleasure to give.

MORE. After you return to Chelsea, send Will to me in London in a few days.

MEG. Will! He's all yours. How on earth can Will help you?

MORE. I need someone I can trust to carry messages. Cromwell has ears, eyes and fingers—so to speak—everywhere. Just for the next few weeks. Someone in the family who can't be corrupted.

MEG. He can't read.

MORE. All the better. He'll memorize.

MEG. Will?! (*Laughs.*) . . . well, you can try.

MORE. There's more to him than we suspect. He must have some spark in that primordial darkness up there if he can love you so. Besides, the line between a village idiot and a stolid citizen is very thin.

MEG. Hmm, yes. Oh, if I were a bit younger! I'd cut my hair, wear a page's clothing, and follow you myself. Alas, now I'd be discovered in a few months' time.

MORE. (*Laughing.*) You have better things to do than stand and wait for me outside the Council chamber rooms.

MEG. Why not use my brother John? Not that I'm disagreeing about Will. . . .

MORE. John's too young; I don't want to interrupt his studies. No, Will will do nicely. Besides, darling,

now that Will is to be father to your children, I'd like
to try and improve him a bit.

MEG. Why? I intend to see to all the business as I
always have.

MORE. It's imprudent should—anything happen to
you. I don't wish to be an alarmist; but Will should
be capable of more than fathering your children.
(*Lightly.*) I'll make a new man of him—

MEG. (*Quietly.*) Of course, dear, as you see fit. I'm
glad if he can help you, of course . . . but his primordial darkness is his chief charm; I worry that education will spoil Will Roper.

MORE. I won't spoil him. Send him up in a few days,
and he and I will return to you before the next chapter
of the family history comes into the world. (*Pause.*)
I had better say goodbye to your mother and my new
son. (*Kissing* MEG.) God bless you; take care of yourself and the family.

MEG. Farewell, Papa. (MEG *watches* MORE *leave.
Then* MEG *turns to us and speaks.*) And so the little
bow-legged scholar leapt onto his impatient steed, and
plunged back into the world of men. And we slowly
wended our way back home by the river—William,
Alice and I. The first few days fled so quickly; I was
not yet accustomed to my newly wed role before I
had to trundle Will back off to London. Oh, those first
few funny days! To lie with Will legally in a big
double bed, toes touching toes! And Mrs. More down
the hall, clenching her hands and clucking her teeth
in the night!

WILL. (*Offstage, calls.*) Meg! Oh, Meg!!

MEG. I'm here, Willy—

WILL. (*He enters, awkwardly, in the same Sunday
suit, with a duffle bag dangling from his hand.*) Do I
look all right, Meg?

MEG. Come here. (WILL *does so sheepishly.*) Your collar's crooked. There. You'll cut quite a figure at court! (MEG *throws her arms around him.*) I'll miss you! It's so wonderful having you scratch my back in the morning, Will.

WILL. (*Earnest.*) I'll always scratch your back, Meg.

MEG. That's very sweet. But, oh, it's not half so exciting as before behind the barn, don't you agree? —Knowing that Mrs. More is listening from the kitchen for twigs snapping, and ready with vengeance and willow switch in hand! Oh, well—those days are gone!

WILL. (*Dismayed.*) I . . . I like it better this way, Meg.

MEG. Now, don't be so glum. I'll get used to it in time. I guess.

WILL. (*Throwing himself on her.*) I don't want to go away from you!

MEG. It's only for a short time. You've never been to stay in town before, have you? (WILL *nods his head "no," fearfully.*) Are you frightened, Will?

WILL. Just . . . a little nervous.

MEG. You'll love it! All the buildings, the noise, the women— (*Teasing.*) Can I let you loose on the town, I wonder.

WILL. You know I'll always be faithful to you, Meg.

MEG. (*Nonchalantly.*) Yes, I know. Be sure to be kind to Papa; he's such a love. You'll adore him when you get to know him better. He's promised to look after you—somehow, in between wet-nursing England, he'll find time for you, too, I suppose. I wish you knew how to write; then you could send me news each day.

WILL. (*Quiet.*) I can.

MEG. (*Stunned.*) What?

WILL. Just a little.

MEG. Will! You never told me that—that you know how to write.

WILL. I can't write anything like you, Meg. (WILL *pulls out some scrawled love poems.*) —But I know how to a little. You'll laugh at my writing . . . (WILL *doesn't give them to her.*)

MEG. No, I won't. (MEG *takes the papers; glancing at them, she smiles.*) We'll write to each other—and then you'll improve yourself in time. I had no idea. (MEG *stares at him in a new light;* ALICE *enters briskly from behind.*)

ALICE. The boat is here and waiting.

WILL. Goodbye, Meg. (WILL *tries to keep a stiff upper lip;* MEG *smiles at his attempt at dignity.*)

MEG. Goodbye, my dear. (WILL *is rigid in front of* ALICE, *but* MEG *kisses him; he turns about, looking stupidly at his right hand, fumbles with his bag, wipes his hands on his trousers, examines his hand again, and then thrusts it nervously at* ALICE.)

WILL. Goodbye, Mrs. More. (*They shake.*)

ALICE. (*Mildly amused.*) Goodbye, William. (WILL *strides from the room.*)

MEG. Well! I suppose I'll miss him.

ALICE. Will you indeed?

MEG. Yes— (*Wickedly.*) I feel as if I've just lost my best hound.

ALICE. (*On cue.*) That's no way to talk about your husband.

MEG. (*Pacing restlessly about.*) Don't you mean that's no way to talk about my hounds? (MEG *turns and catches* ALICE *with a faint smile on her face, which*

ALICE *quickly suppresses*.) Oocch— My back hurts already—

ALICE. You'd better start keeping off your feet. It's going to get much worse before getting better.

MEG. (*Marches to table and sits.*) I should be glad to have an excuse to sit and read; but I feel so restless for some reason.

ALICE. That, too, will get worse before getting better. Do you mind if I stay here and knit?

MEG. (*Surprised.*) Please do— (ALICE *takes knitting out of her apron, and sits promptly at the other chair. Then she begins to knit seriously and furiously—just as she does everything else.* MEG *pretends to read, but can't concentrate.* MEG *watches* ALICE *instead.*) Um— what are you knitting?

ALICE. A bonnet—can't you tell? (ALICE *holds it up for* MEG *to inspect.*)

MEG. That's very nice—but I don't know anything about knitting. (*Sheepish.*) I never learned.

ALICE. With your father's priorities, that fails to surprise me. (*A pause ensues.*)

MEG. Do you like to knit?

ALICE. I never thought about it. (*She stops to think.*) I think it's more a habit than a hobby. It's rather like saying beads—one's thoughts wander and stray.

MEG. What do you think about when you knit?

ALICE. (*Amused.*) You must be bored to be asking *me* questions.

MEG. No, please. . . .

ALICE. Well—mostly I remember my father, the house where I was born. . . . I don't like to think of my first husband much. Just patches, really—nothing profound or scholarly. I guess I think of my mother most often—she taught me to knit when I was very young; we spent hours together at night in front of the fire.

MEG. You've never told me about your mother. What was she like?

ALICE. (*Uneasy at being asked questions.*) She was just an ordinary woman. She worked hard; and she never complained.

MEG. Yes, but what was she like?

ALICE. I really don't know. She never talked much. (*Quickly.*) But she was a good mother—stern, didn't spoil us none—any. She couldn't read, but she made sure we knew our catechism. And she checked behind our ears twice a year or so, as all mothers should—and as I hope you'll do to your children.

MEG. (*Smiling.*) If I should forget to check behind their ears, you'll remind me, won't you? Was she pretty?

ALICE. Excuse me?

MEG. Your mother—was she pretty?

ALICE. (*Pleased that* MEG *is taking an interest.*) Well, now, that depends on what you mean by pretty. (*Harder.*) None of my family had looks that would attract attention. We're all of us plain. (*But she softens.*) But I think my mother was pretty; soft in her face—or anyhow, that's how I remember her, how soft she was by the fire, teaching me to knit. (*She pauses.*) I often think: your father's going to be a famous man, Meg. His name will go down in books, and others will read them, and know of his existence. And even you, wasting your eyes, can pass down the things you've written; you'll be remembered, too. All I have from my mother is a dim recollection of her face—which gets blurred with each year. And I still have all the clothes she's knitted for me. Still have every stitch. They're sturdy.

MEG. That's really all women have to be remembered by—each stitch a mute word to testify that they existed in the first place. . . .

ALICE. (*Enraptured that* MEG *has transformed her thoughts into eloquence; then back down to earth.*) —Well, I don't know if I would say it that way—I mean, there's always children.

MEG. How did—how did your mother die?

ALICE. (*Matter of fact.*) How do most women die? In child-bed.

MEG. Like my mother. In child-bed.

ALICE. (*With authority.*) Well, you're not to worry. Nothing will happen to you. The first one's the most difficult, but the least dangerous. And you're strong, and young, and stubborn—just as I was when I had my first.

MEG. (*Trying to sound brave.*) Oh, I'm not the least concerned. Besides, I've been reading up on it. I borrowed Dr. Lacomb's medical tract; there's a section on deliveries. . . .

ALICE. Ttissh! What do doctors know? (*Curious.*) What does it say?

MEG. Let me see—I'll try to translate—Um—"During pains a" a young?—no a "virgin dove should be secured to—to the feet to draw humours from the womb"—

ALICE. —Stuff and nonsense! Doctors aren't fit to extract teeth or lance pimples! Virgin doves, indeed! Hah! We'll see that you have all that you need; there's nothing to learn from book-lore! A midwife and a strong rope, that's the answer—

MEG. (*Nervously.*) A strong rope?

ALICE. Aye— (ALICE *winds up her knitting.*) You can pull on it and sing out plainsong. I'll bring up tea— (ALICE *exits.*)

MEG. (*She closes the book, and speaks to us.*) Alice More was right. Not all the book-lore in the world could help me keep the life within me. Having changed its mind, it struggled to leave before its time had come. My child—and somehow I know it would have been a girl—my daughter departed, wisely deciding to wait another century or so. (*There is a spot in front of the Tower, in which* SIR THOMAS *stands.*) From my father in London: (MEG *is disturbed.*) hastily written words of . . . of comfort, and love, and. . . .

MORE and MEG. (*Simultaneously.*) There will be others, Meg. There will be others.

MEG. (*Alone.*) There would be.

ALICE. (*She enters with a mug of tea.*) So—you're up and about again, Meg? Is that wise?

MEG. I was bored in bed. I wanted to be up and doing; so I thought I'd check in on the school and see how their studies were progressing.

ALICE. That's precisely what you shouldn't be doing. It's all that book-lore that caused the babe to drop in the first place. It's been proven that women must rest before a birth; you should not have been scribbling and reading—

MEG. —Since when have you been a believer in medical science? You know very well that cooks and charmaids and farmers' wives clean and sweep and sweat up to the last moment; can the exercise of one's fingers in turning over the page be more strenuous? I refuse to believe that one.

ALICE. Well, don't be cross with me. I'm merely trying to fulfill the promise I made to your father before he left to see that you rest and leave the books alone for a while. There's nothing for you to do right now; the new tutor doesn't need any of your help; you'll only undermine his authority. And it seems to me you should conserve your strength for your husband's arrival; he's a strain enough. . . .

MEG. Oh, Will. I don't think it necessary to send him all the way from London. There is no danger. For heaven's sake, why all the fuss?

ALICE. He'll only be here for the weekend; it's more for his peace of mind and your father's than for your own. I thought you'd be a bit more eager to see him.

MEG. (*She pauses, wondering whether or not to confide.*) Well— I feel uneasy about him. (ALICE *looks at* MEG *quizzically.*) It's just that his letters are so strange—not like him at all. It makes me frightened. (*Quiet.*) I'm very frightened.

ALICE. (*Touched.*) Well, lit'racy's not the french pox, is it? Suppose your scribbling had frightened him off?

MEG. It's just that I don't know him at all. At all. (MEG *laughs.*) I thought there was nothing to know!

ALICE. The strongest marriages are built on total ignorance. So Will has a mind underneath it all—I find it hard to believe; but it could be worse—

MEG. That's what is so strange—his letters are scrawls; misspelled, smudged—as if written with perspiration and knotted tongue. He's trying so hard—

ALICE. Do his letters make any sense?

MEG. In a· bizarre way. His letters are still simpleminded, but simpleminded with a purpose. They're all one long string of misspelled platitudes—but whose platitudes, I wonder?

ALICE. There's nothing wrong with platitudes; some might be better off if they followed 'em. What kinds of things does he say?

MEG. Oh, he's filled with talk ·about "stumping out heresy."

ALICE. Stumping?

MEG. It rather sounds as if he proposes to amputate the devil. . . .

ALICE. (*Cautiously.*) Meg—before Will arrives— would you mind a bit of womanly advice? I do not think it advisable that you two should . . . well, should—that is, please be careful not to—

MEG. —not to what?

ALICE. (*Blushing.*) To fulfill your wifely duty.

MEG. (*Struck.*) Well, of course not. I have no inclination for "Wifely duty," right now. Of course, the irony is that one's inclination for wifely duty diminishes after marriage. . . .

ALICE. Be that as it may, it really is a bit soon; you need time to recover and you must make your husband understand that you need bed-rest—

MEG. Will has never had any say in these matters. He'll agree of course.

ALICE. I would not intrude if it were not for the fact that such female weakness runs in your family.

MEG. In my family!

ALICE. (*Quickly.*) Your mother had her last child too soon—

MEG. Yes, I know. The familiar story of too many too soon. But she wanted another child; as it was her choice, it was her risk.

ALICE. (*Questioningly.*) Was it?

MEG. Yes! Father has often told me how guilty he feels for letting mother persuade him.

ALICE. The last child was a son—an only son.

MEG. I do not understand.

ALICE. Perhaps it's just as well. (ALICE *picks up* MEG's *mug of tea.*) I'd better see after our supper—

MEG. —No! Please explain what—

ALICE. —there's nothing to explain. (ALICE *starts to*

exit; on her cross WILL *enters. He stands erect, impressive in simple but well-cut clothes.*) Well!

WILL. (*He bows handsomely; takes* ALICE's *hand, kisses it gallantly, and murmurs:*) Madam. (*Then his head bobs up, with an idiotic grin.*) I-I learnt that at court, Mmmrs. More.

ALICE. (*Astonished, jerks her hand away.*) Stuff and Nonsense! That passes for a gentlemen's education, I suppose. Your wife is in there—go slobber on her hand. (ALICE *goes to her bench.*)

WILL. (*Behind* MEG's *back.*) Wife. (WILL *bends and kisses her neck.*)

MEG. Will! You—you startled me. Well, let's take a look at you—yes, you're quite improved. Your collar's straight.

WILL. (*Throws himself down beside her.*) I've been so worried, Meg. God has spared you; I-I intend to—to take care of you, y'see. Not, uh, not shirk my husbandly duty anymore; become a new man. Yes, a new man, and—well, take care of you.

MEG. (*Trying not to appear upset.*) Stuff and Nonsense, as Alice would say; I'm really perfectly capable of taking care of myself, Will. I've had a minor upset; but I'm recovering quickly—nourished on the bouillion of everyone's platitudes. I don't need care taken of me.

WILL. But I want to. Your father says I'm to return on weekends to—to look after you—until he can return. And then, he says, we'll all begin again—to study and fulfill our—our missions.

MEG. Willy! Our missions! What mission could you possibly have? Other than scratching my back in the morning.

WILL. (*Earnest.*) This is not a subject for levitation. . . .

MEG. Levitation?

WILL. I'm just a simple man, I-I know. But every man has a mission to follow. I think my mission is to help your father fulfill his.

MEG. (*Thunderstruck.*) You! Will Roper! Help Sir Thomas! What mission does he have that you can help him with?

WILL. Your father is a great man. (*Pompously.*) A great man.

MEG. I don't quite know why it irritates me so to hear those words in other people's mouths. But it does, Will. Who knows his greatness better than I? But to hear others cant about the greatness of Sir Thomas More— (*Quickly.*) I don't think I want to know about the greatness you mean. His greatness is here—here at Chelsea, with his family, his books, his small community of neighbours. He has the greatness of quiet and calm; exposure to the world of Cromwell's can only tarnish his greatness. He should come home—his place is here.

(MEG *and* WILL *are silent a moment.*)

WILL. I don't agree. His gifts should be shared. (MEG *is about to speak.*) —But I didn't come from London to argue with you. (MEG *stares.*) I—I don't mean to upset you, Meg. I want to wait 'til you are well again, and then we c'n talk . . . you don't look very good at all. Why don't you rest? (WILL *pats* MEG *clumsily.*) That's why I'm here . . . to see that you rest. . . . So, you rest—and while you're resting, I'll go and get you some t-t-tea. . . . (WILL *exits.*)

MEG. (*To audience.*) Each weekend thereafter he came to me, to see, ostensibly, that I "rested"—he kept me in bed, at any rate; hiding his husbandly desire beneath husbandly solicitude. And I? Rather than endure his newly-found philosophy, I gave in—like many a wife, I stopped his chatter by channeling his expression elsewhere. I was not allowed to remain barren for long. In a few weeks, my father returned at last from London; by the time he came, I again had news with which to greet him. (MORE *enters upstage;* MEG *runs to* MORE *and they embrace:*)

MORE. Greetings, my love.

MEG. Ah! The return of the prodigal father!

MORE. Why am I prodigal?

MEG. It's a very great sin that you've kept away from us so long, father.

MORE. But now I'm home. You're looking almost well again.

MEG. I've been well for weeks!

MORE. And you—did you miss me, Meg?

MEG. I've practically pined, father. You know that.

MORE. (*Pleased.*) Your letters were my only solace.

MEG. And you—did you miss me?

MORE. Of course. It's been a long, busy time. We have lots of things to talk about, and I have a lot of schemes—

MEG. —but I have news for you, too, Papa. I am again with child.

MORE. Again? Son Roper wastes no time, does he? (MORE *sniggers à la Cromwell's "Anne Boleyn" jokes— he catches himself, and adjusts his persona. Then, gently:)* I'm delighted, Meg—and very concerned. This time we will be very careful.

MEG. I'm fine.

MORE. Ah, but this time no studies, no teaching. We can't afford to take chances—

MEG. I will go mad without books and teaching, Papa!

MORE. Please, Meg—I promise that Will and I will

distract you; I fear your constant activity will be harmful to your health. And I could not bear should anything happen to you, too— (*They look at each other.*) It's only for a short time, Meg; for my sake?

MEG. For your sake.

MORE. Besides, there's plenty for you to do in the month ahead! But before I go into all that—what do you think of Will?

MEG. He's—well, he's certainly changed.

MORE. (*Proud.*) Yes, is he not! A new man! He and I have decided— The King is calling a new parliament; we need someone to challenge the county seat for the House of Commons—

MEG. (*Horror.*) You can't mean—you're not actually saying— (MEG *peals laughter.*) I see! Pulling my leg again, Papa! I actually thought for a moment that you were proposing that Will should run for Parliament.

MORE. I mean exactly that.

MEG. Oh, God.

MORE. Now Meg—give the man some credit. Besides, he's really standing in for me. . . .

MEG. A vote for William Roper is a vote for Thomas More?

MORE. (*Modest.*) He only needs a little coaching. . . .

(ALICE *enters with* WILL *in tow, in his familiar Sunday suit.* MORE *and* MEG *converge on him; the three of them push and prod* WILL *downstage; counsel him, straighten his collar, comb back his hair . . . and then group behind him, to his left. He faces stage right, and begins to speak; as he does so, he spasmodically twitches:*)

WILL. M-M-my good people: (*He pauses, and stops his knees from violently trembling.*) These, are, uh, are, um, doubled tries—I mean, troubled times— (*He perspires.*) as we all, uh, know. Those of us with l-l-land must, um, hoard—no, ah, "safeguard" uh, the g-greatness of England; and we can do this best by—by—by— (*Pause.*) protecting our breasted—no!—vested interests. (*ALICE, MEG and MORE have been active spectators to all this; at this point they converge on WILL again—the director may choose to use a bell, as in boxing rounds, to separate the speeches. MEG and ALICE comb back his hair, which has become wild; straighten his jacket, pull up his pants, wipe his face, etc.—while MORE consults with him and pats his back. . . . Round Two—the three withdraw into the background to watch avidly; WILL takes courage, a deep breath, and pivots to face stage left. He becomes a bit more relaxed, and grows in fervour throughout:*) I come here today to bore—uh, implore you to-to-search your cun-cun-conscience! Luther's power is growing a-a-broad; we are in-infested (*He violently slaps himself and then scratches the spot.*) from within by Hair-es-y!! (*Growing more and more evangelical.*) Extreme measures are c-called for! We must burn heretical books! Burn Heretics! Split Hairs!! (*Immediate end of Round Two—again the family cuts him off, and overwhelm him, not quite pleased with his preaching style. They coax, rub, pat, and unrumple him. Round Three is about to begin. He faces front, completely cold, disinterested, boring and pedantic. The Polished Spokesman: we see at last the WILLIAM ROPER who will write the famous MORE biography.*) The issues I stand for are clear, gentlemen. I appeal to your reason and your stout, loyal hearts. I mean to fight heretical d-dissension, and strengthen the position of the landed gentry. Our interests, our taxes, our pastures best serve the King, God and Country. With zeal, modesty, and Sir Thomas More's monies, I stand before you, eager to serve: For the Church, King Henry, and Free Rights to Pasture!! (*The* MORE *family politely, but enthusiastically, applauds.*)

END OF ACT TWO

ACT THREE

At the opening of the act, MORE *is sitting at the table, to the right. At the other end of the table,* WILL *is seated. There are quills and ink wells in front of each.* MORE *is working; there is a large stack of paper in front of him, and he scribbles furiously, turning pages. At the other end of the table is an identical stack of papers for* WILL. *At curtain rise, however,* WILL *sits with furrowed brow, deep in contemplation. In the stillness we can almost hear his wheels sluggishly churning in his mind; we hear the frantic scratch of pen on paper.* MEG *stands downstage, towards us:*

MEG. After William Roper's victorious conquest of his parliament seat, the lights in my father's study burned through the nights. Side by side they sat, the bow-legged scholar and the village idiot, preparing William Roper to plunge into the world of men. And I? I walked the corridors of the house, feeling orphaned without book, father and husband. (MEG *turns, and enters the study area hesitantly from the right:*) Am I intruding? (MORE, *oblivious, scratches on.*)

WILL. (*Importantly.*) I'm helping your father with his tracks.

MEG. With his what? Father—what is this about?

MORE. What? (MORE *absentmindedly surfaces from his paper.*) Oh—did I neglect to tell you, Meg? When I met Cardinal Campeggio in London, he brought a

56

message from the Pope— (*Confidentially.*) could I use my—and I quote—my "considerable literary gifts" to instruct rather than entertain? Refutations of Luther's heretical tracts are urgently needed; it is His Holiness' request that I write in behalf of Rome.

MEG. (*Quietly.*) Oh. (MEG *straightens herself, cheerfully brisk.*) Well, then, how may I assist?

MORE. Many thanks, dear, but I have all the assistance I need— (MORE *indicates* WILL, *slowly laboring at the other end of the table.*)

MEG. Will is assisting you! How—?!

MORE. (*To* MEG, *amused.*) Sh! Go and see— (MEG *tiptoes over to stand behind* WILL'S *shoulder, peers over, and watches him.* WILL *picks up a pen, peruses the page, and carefully makes a notation on the sheet —he examines his work critically, flips the page over, and passes to the next.*)

MEG. (*Smiling.*) Oh. He's numbering pages. (*Relieved,* MEG *asks again a bit pleading.*) Are you sure there is no way I can help?

MORE. I should have thought, Meg, that you would not be so eager to defend Church orthodoxy—and that Luther did not concern you.

MEG. It's true that I do not care one way or the other about Luther. I follow the conventions of the Church because it is easiest for me. Why dissent when dissent itself comes from belief?

MORE. I had best do this work myself.

MEG. Yes. But I'd like to read your tracts when you finish writing—may I? (MORE *nods assent.*) Good. Now, what should I do with myself? No teaching, no books—and alas— (MEG *looks at* WILL, *sitting there poised and pompous.*) no barn bundling either!

MORE. There is something you could do to help us in terms of Will's political image. It is tradition that

the parliament member's wife attends to the alms
house for the aged.

MEG. The alms house? In the village? (*Shudders.*)
What good can I do there?

MORE. It's a gesture . . . and—and you may enjoy
it.

MEG. What can be enjoyable about charity? I've
never had a taste for leper-kissing—but I'll go—not
to discover my "mission"—but for your sakes. (WILL
stands, and hands MEG *a hooded cloak and basket.
She slowly walks around the stage to the right, in a
circle.*) I went to the alms house—and there received
the deference of the toothless. The old men, gasping
for breath, stood with some hidden reserve of strength
as I passed; the women blessed me, and my father,
and my husband. Imbecilic smiles of gratitude
twisted their faces: "Oh, my lady! The honor! So
like her father!" And they pressed my hands, and
received the meager hand-outs of apples they could
not chew, and the stockings which would slide down
their bony legs. I saw my reflection in their eyes:
Thomas More's daughter, William Roper's wife.
(*Quietly.*) Perhaps that was the most sobering sight
of all. I could not return. (MEG *throws off her cloak
and storms back to the study, where* MORE *still scribbles furiously, and* WILL *is intensely examining the
written sheets.*) Papa!

WILL. (*He looks up from his labor.*) Oh, back so
soon, Meg?

MEG. Father—I went to the alms house—

MORE. (*Still writing, and flipping pages onto the
floor; absently.*) Oh, did you? How was it?

MEG. Very upsetting, Papa. I felt so—so hypocritical,
so mean. To think that some ladies go once a week on
such errands of mercy, and return to their families

feeling uplifted, secure in their salvation, complacent in their youth and well-being. Accepting the curtsies of the arthritic as their due homage! Christian charity such as that is nothing more than a mirror—a mirror of one's own good opinion of one's self! I'm sorry, Papa—I can't return there. It shames me.

MORE. (*Totally oblivious.*) That's nice—I'm glad you enjoyed yourself.

MEG. (*She is silent. She endeavors to shake off her hurt, and in an attempt at cheerfulness:*) And—and how is your work progressing?

MORE. (*With satisfaction.*) Rapidly—I think we should have an effective refutation to Luther on the Continent within weeks.

WILL. (*Impressively.*) I'm on page nineteen.

MEG. (*Picking up a page.*) May I? (MORE *nods. She scans it quickly—and frowns.*)

MORE. (*Quickly.*) Why do you frown?

MEG. It's—it's not exactly your best work, Papa. I am not struck by the force of your style here; it reads rather like a barrister's tome—

MORE. How else should one refute heresy than by logic?

MEG. (*Smiling ironically.*) Perhaps; still and all, this work does not seem worthy of you, Papa. Your name will not be remembered for these words here.

MORE. No, not by this will my name live on.

(CROMWELL *has entered behind them;* CROMWELL *bears a long, dark crimson robe; over his arm we catch the glitter of a golden chain.*)

CROMWELL. Sir Thomas: Cardinal Woolsey is dead. (*They all start and stare at* MORE, *the most thunderstruck*—MORE *glances at the robe, and surmises at once—a wonder, a joy, glows on his face;* MORE *leaps up, and mastering himself, cries out in stern tones—*)

MORE. God rest his soul. (*Crosses himself.*)

CROMWELL. (*Decorously crossing himself, as the others do.*) Of course. (CROMWELL *waits.*) His Majesty asks that you leave off your writings for actions once more, and serve the King as Chancellor.

MORE. His Grace is too good; I am not worthy of this office.

MEG. The office is not worthy of you—

CROMWELL. For a layman, the office of Chancellor is the most exalted in the realm. Would you care to explain yourself, Mistress Roper?

WILL. (*Hastily.*) M-my wife means that—

MEG. What does Sir Thomas sacrifice in taking office? Will His Majesty be understanding about my father's stand . . . of not taking a stand . . . in the marriage question?

CROMWELL. His Majesty respects your father's wish to remain a dutiful son of Rome; he will respect your father's conscience in all matters.

MEG. Then is His Majesty cruel. The King will play cat and mouse with you, father; please—do not take the office if you can not bend your will to the King's.

WILL. It is your duty to take office; to translate your vision through deeds. You must—

CROMWELL. (*Sharing* MEG'S *inability to listen to* WILL *for long, he cuts* WILL *off.*) —The King wishes it.

MORE. Then—then I will.

(MEG *turns away quietly;* CROMWELL *and* WILL *help* MORE *into the gown, and slip the chain over his head. The gown should be padded and full-length, to transform withered scholars into massive figures*

*of state. MEG looks back at the finished effect,
and involuntarily cries:*)

MEG. Your legs! They're completely covered, Papa;
those dear orphan legs. . . .
MORE. This is not a subject for levity. . . .

(*The two men step back from MORE; CROMWELL bows
and withdraws, WILL goes back to the table and
sits: during the next monologue MORE completes
a sweeping, slow circle towards stage right, towards the Tower, and then back again, in increas-
ingly ponderous steps.*)

MEG. (*She faces the audience and chronicles:*) My
father's reign as Chancellor would not last long; long
enough for his fame to spread, but not long enough
for the golden chain to become tinsel to his eyes. The
marriage of Anne and Henry grew ever more urgent
as His Majesty's desire grew: in a monotonous refrain,
the King first questioned, then requested, then de-
manded. The Pope refused annulment, and Sir
Thomas retreated behind the shadow of the Pope . . .
until at last, King Henry divorced the Church itself.
An Act Of Supremacy was placed in front of Parliament: The King declared the Head of the Church in
England by oath of every subject. (MORE *and* WILL
face each other, and speak over MEG's *monologue:*)
MEG and MORE. (*Unison.*) And the penalty?
MEG and WILL. High treason.
MORE. (*Alone.*) High treason. (MORE *fingers his
chain.*) I had better take this off, then, Son Roper, had
I not? I do not want it melted down in the flames—
WILL. You will not take the oath? (*Triumphant.*)

I knew you would not! Now we fight for principles as men!

MEG. (*Rushing in.*) Father! You will not take the oath?

WILL. Of course not.

MORE. I intend to take off my chain of office.

MEG. (*Pleading.*) Oh, no—no, do not. Once I pleaded with you not to put on that chain unless you were willing to bend. That is the only duty of Chancellors—they must sway according.to a King's whimsey. You accepted that responsibility to efface your own dignity to the King's. Now swallow your pride, and bend, Father. You must bend—or burn.

MORE. I can not swear the Oath—although I will not swear against it. To me, the Pope will ever be the Supreme Head of the Church. These are mere words to you, Meg—but they are conventions by which I have lived.

MEG. The only convention we live by is fear—(*Angry.*) we live by the convention of groveling . . . the humble man who would both serve his fellow man and love his family is he who stoops lowest. Had you remained home, you could have kept your honor in obscurity.

MORE. Since I left home for the King's service, I have become convinced in the necessity for order. Pope must follow Pope as heirs to St. Peter, just as son must follow father. There is a hierarchy which is ordained; and in this vast chain, I can not follow my own will. I am but a tool.

MEG. —Think of your wife; think of your children who must suffer for the danger you put them in if you should defy the King.

WILL. (*Stepping between them and upstaging* MEG.)

I can speak for your family— Give us an example to follow.

MORE. (*He hesitates; then with pomp solemnity, he removes the chain of office from around his neck.*) My children: here is an end to any discussion of divorces, marriages, kings or churches. I put them all away from me, and seek refuge in silence. No one must know my mind as to the oath—neither you, Meg— (*Warmly.*) nor even you, Son Roper, a true son of the Church. (*Lighter.*) We will talk about the weather. Under the law, "silence is consent."

MEG. My silence shall be rebellion shouted. (*MEG breaks away from the two and walks right.*)

MORE. Will: take this to Cromwell and beg His Majesty to release me from service.

(*WILL takes the chain to the right where CROMWELL waits, then rejoins MORE. CROMWELL holds the chain up to the light, smiles, and puts it on as a vain woman would a bauble. MEG, who has broken away from MORE and WILL and moved down stage, is passed by CROMWELL as he crosses the stage towards MORE. As CROMWELL passes:*)

CROMWELL. The wheels spin once more, Mistress Roper.

MEG. (*She starts—sees him; for once letting down her defences, MEG says sadly.*) Yes—that must give you a great deal of pleasure, Master Cromwell.

CROMWELL. I am not so simplistic as to be amused by the downfall of others; I am pleased in so far as my predictions are proved accurate. Your father is quite predictable—and so, no threat to me.

MEG. I did not foresee this.

CROMWELL. No—of course not. (*Right now* MASTER CROMWELL *is in an expansive mood.*) You proved right, madam on the matters of the policy of Rome—we can always analyze matters which touch us little—but to analyze one's father— (MEG *silently waits for him to leave.*) If I may suggest your mistake in perception —you see your father in terms of one role and one face—ah, do we not all see our fathers so? But he has many faces. A politician must always understand that people are composites—and play these composites of individuals against others—and even against themselves.

MEG. (*Disturbed and wary.*) Why are you telling me all this, sir?

CROMWELL. I? Only as a friendly gesture. I do not know you, Mistress Meg—or should I say, I only know that side of you revealed by Sir Thomas. The side of the devoted daughter.

MEG. My father has talked of me to you?

CROMWELL. In his London days his greatest joy was to read aloud your letters to him—exemplary letters of devotion. (CROMWELL *studies the effect of this on her.*) I hope that Meg Roper has other sides to her— for her own sake.

MEG. (*Defiant once more.*) Gracious thanks for your tactful hint. I am sure that now, sir, we will move in different spinning circles—you, Chancellor at court, and we, private subjects at Chelsea. We will see each other no longer. Farewell.

CROMWELL. Oh, no, madam—I am sure we will see each other again in the future— (*Smiling, he bows;* CROMWELL *walks to* WILL *and* MORE, *and politely bows to* MORE. *They have been waiting for him. Together the three men walk to the Tower in a procession.* WILL *and* CROMWELL *wheel out a small scaffold;* MORE *with*

dignity directs their labors. Once the scaffold is posi-
tioned, the men bow to each other again. MORE *climbs*
the stair to a small stool, which is spotlighted; with
noble expression he waits upon the stool. CROMWELL
exits; WILL *regards* MORE *as Moslems contemplate the*
east.)

MEG. (*Having watched the dumbshow with us, she*
wearily speaks.) And now the days of persecution began. Father remained in the Tower, and Will became
a pilgrim to his cell. As for Chelsea—the servants were
released, and the school disbanded. Our revenues and
monies were seized by the state. Inflicted with the
plague of the King's displeasure, we remained within
doors, friendless and isolated. (MEG *walks to an area*
where ALICE *sits, darning clothes. Picking up a bucket,*
she carefully wipes the bottom of her shoes on an edge
of the platform.)

ALICE. Meg? Wipe your feet before you enter the
kitchen—

MEG. (*Eyes raised in resignation against mothers.*)
Yes, I will.

ALICE. (*Making room for* MEG *to sit down on the*
bench.) Did you milk the cow, then?

MEG. (*Flopping down with relief.*) Yes—she's getting used to me, I think. (MEG *looks at her hands.*)
And I'm beginning to get the knack. Half of it man-
aged to hit the pail today. Aren't you cold, just sitting
here? Your hands must be numb. Should I put another
log on the fire?

ALICE. Not for my sake. We've got to conserve. Your
father's far colder where he is—

MEG. —my father chose to be cold. I did not.

ALICE. Your father is a good man.

MEG. Is he a good husband? (*They exchange glances;*
ALICE *looks away.*)

ALICE. You must make allowances for him.

MEG. I have no patience for martyrs. (*Pause.*) Lately I find myself wondering what my parents' marriage was really like—

ALICE. (*Quietly.*) I'm sure your mother loved your father.

MEG. Did she? He claims to have absolutely worshipped her—am I bothering you with such prattle?

ALICE. Of course not. . . . (*But we see her hands fumble with the thread.*)

MEG. (*Casually, baiting* ALICE.) Yes—he's forever sermonizing on how exquisite Jane Colt was: how as a young barrister he visited John Colt's estate and fell instantly in love with her—

ALICE. (*Falling for the bait, she outs with:*) He did not. He fell in love with Jane Colt's younger sister. He only married your mother because she was eldest. (*With irrepressible human nature.*) —She was also plainer. . . .

MEG. (*Amused.*) Did Father tell you this?

ALICE. No—but I knew her slightly—only by sight. She came to town monthly to visit the alms house. And then there were tales, of course. (*A bit bitter.*) There are always tales about women married to prominent men.

MEG. (*Earnest.*) Tell me—was my mother very like me? Father always swears I take after her—in appearance, in intelligence, in temperament . . . do I?

ALICE. Heavens, I only knew the lady by sight. (*Sarcastic.*) We hardly moved in the same circles then. But—I will tell you one more tale—only one more. Some say that when Jane Colt left her father's house she left it as a simple country girl, unlearned and rustic. Your father had some funny notions at that time that women should be companions—and mistresses of fine art—or some such nonsense! And so he tutored his newly wed in reading, and made her practise the lute, and Latin and what not. Well, Jane More would rather have swept floors than become some dancing dog—and your father was as stern as only the young with new ideas can be. She stopped eating. And some say she pounded her head against the floor in fits, rather than read. Some say your father had to lock her in—but that she escaped anyway, and ran home to her father's house—and Master Colt took her by the hand and dragged her back—giving her a scolding as to a wife's duty. I suppose your father gave up his experimenting; at any rate she soon had five children. So much for Latin!

MEG. (*Astounded.*) So the story of my mother's refinements is a myth!

ALICE. Well—a myth told with love.

MEG. Weren't you afraid to marry him after all this? That he would force you to recite poetry on your wedding night?

ALICE. I was set in my ways by the time your father got to me. (*Humbly.*) He never even tried with me. . . . (*Stronger, she pushes away her self-pity.*) And with your sisters and brother to look after, I had enough on my hands. . . .

MEG. Why?—

ALICE. —Did I marry him? (*Agitated, quick.*) Because he did me the honor to ask me. I could hardly believe my ears—he a distinguished man—me a merchant's widow, with my children grown, and my looks gone—and then, he needed help with five of his own—and he was such a good man—and I felt so sorry for him, with his wife so recently gone—

MEG. Recently gone? You were our housekeeper for over a year before you married my father—

ALICE. Oh, yes. That's what I meant. (ALICE *is silent, thinking something over—and then she decides. With eyes averted,* ALICE *softly says.*) That's not what I meant. Meg—you have no idea of my love for your father. It's time you learn. For all these years, I have appeared to you as a hard, unloving wife. But that is not the truth. I, too, have sacrificed— (*Quickly.*) we married within a month of your mother's death—

MEG. What! What are you saying . . . !

ALICE. I wasn't his housekeeper alone; we married at night in secrecy. And I—I for love of him kept quiet until time could elapse. (*Simply.*) That is how much I love your father.

MEG. (*Holding onto the bench beneath her.*) He— he married you only a month after!! After my mother —his beloved wife . . . and you agreed to—to come and wash our clothes and be his wife to him at night! Knowing that he was, was— (MEG *trails off.*)

ALICE. He was ashamed of me. Yes—at first. But he needed someone. I was glad to be the one.

MEG. And all to save appearances! (MEG *rises, shaken.*) Thank you for telling me all this. (MEG *touches* ALICE's *shoulder.*) I should not have any—any illusions.

ALICE. It's right that you should know—I will be in my room should you need me— (ALICE *goes to the upstage area;* MEG *stands very still, with her head turned in the direction of* ALICE's *exit. Then, wearily, she turns to us:*)

MEG. There comes a time in life when father and daughter turn round and see each other as man and woman. (*Pause.*) Both diminish in size. (MEG *walks to the step, sits, and leans forward towards us; seized by her revery, she bursts forth with:*) —Once as a child on my father's estate, I raced to the river to watch

October skies float downstream. Hour upon hour I sat in rapt discussion with the fall, my blood coursing in currents. As I gazed up at that limitless, eternal October blue, I can remember thinking: "That is how much I love my father." (*Her revery gently disintegrates; she rises and says.*) Now seasons and men can no longer move me, and I can barely remember my great child's love for Sir Thomas, as withered as the memory of a child's October. (MEG *walks stage right and discovers* CROMWELL, *browsing through the family biography; she stops, as he sees her.*)

CROMWELL. Please—do come in.

MEG. My husband is not at home.

CROMWELL. No, I know he's not. I believe he's keeping an eye on the Tower for us right now. I came to talk with you. It would do me no earthly good to talk with Master Roper. (MEG *is silent; he returns to the book.*) All of your family history is very diverting; I must take it back with me, I'm afraid. Yes, I must appropriate all of Sir Thomas' writings.

MEG. Please—help yourself.

CROMWELL. How very good of you. While I am sorting this morass out, you might be so good as to look something over— (*From within his cloak* CROMWELL *removes a paper which he gives to* MEG; *he picks up the sheets of paper as she reads.*)

MEG. (*Still.*) You are not seriously suggesting that I turn state evidence against my own father. . . .

CROMWELL. I am indeed.

MEG. First I would have to perjure myself; secondly, I could never turn against my own father—you know I can not do this.

CROMWELL. I do not know—I predict. I predict that before I leave here it will be with your signature on that paper. And for some very good reasons. All I need is your signed testimony that your father, in front of you, swore against the King's supremacy. You did not read further of conditions of your testimony: may I save you the effort of reading? (MEG *nods*.) First, no one—including your father—will know of your testimony—only the closed court will know: secondly, all records will be destroyed. And we are prepared to grant certain immunities—

MEG. Such as?

CROMWELL. Your husband has refused to take the oath. We will not prosecute him—we want martyrs such as your father, not imitative madmen. And for the rest of his natural life, William Roper may expose his heresy as men with perversions expose themselves in public—without suffering serious harm. I believe you yourself are with child, madam?

MEG. Yes. (MEG *turns herself away from his gaze*.)

CROMWELL. Your family will not suffer unduly—although your father's lands are forfeit, your husband's land will not be; and the crown will not extend its displeasure to your children—or to your siblings who are all under legal age. Provided they remain sensible, quiet citizens, of course.

MEG. Go on.

CROMWELL. There are other immediate benefits for your testimony—ones that I think will be the most appealing. Your signature will save your father from unnecessary discomfort—if we convict him with your assistance, the unpleasant means of torture will be waived by the prosecutor. And lastly—Sir Thomas will be quickly, quietly, and humanely executed—there will be little wait. As a last indulgence of affection, His Majesty will commute the sentence from burning alive at the stake to death by beheading—a small detail that your father might appreciate.

MEG. (*Exhausted.*) I want my family to be left alone in peace.

CROMWELL. We want the same, then. The King wants an effective, immediate example made to uphold the oath. Your father, it seems, dearly wants to be that example. In signing this, you answer his prayer.

MEG. But—but I never heard my father deny Henry's supremacy. . . .

CROMWELL. Think again, Meg. (*He waits.*)

MEG. Perhaps he did speak slightingly of the King's supremacy. . . .

CROMWELL. (*Taking pen.*) That will do. . . .

MEG. If I sign today, when—

CROMWELL. —He will be executed tomorrow morning. (*Gently.*) And now you will sign—both sides of you. One side will sign out of compassion. The other side will sign out of retaliation. (*Grandly.*) Our motives are always mixed.

MEG. Spare me your penetrating analysis, Sir. (*She stops with the pen.*) Are you not afraid, Master Cromwell, of my signature? Someday your daughters, if only in the dark of their minds, will sign a piece of parchment condemning you, too, to mortality. . . . (*Sadly, to herself.*) I should, for love of him, for love of all fathers, lay down this pen. . . . (*As she reflects,* CROMWELL *barely breathes.*) But I can not martyr myself for the memory of October— (*Decisively.*) I will sign. (MEG *does so, and* CROMWELL, *in relief, snatches up the paper.*)

CROMWELL. (*Gathering up the papers and the book.*) Thank you. And now I am sure we will not meet again— (CROMWELL *leaves and strides towards the Tower, browsing through the book. Deciding it is worthless,* CROMWELL *hands the book back to* MORE— *and exits with the papers.* WILL *rushes to the study.*)

WILL. Meg! They are executing him tomorrow—

MEG. —I know.

WILL. How can you—?

MEG. —It doesn't matter how. (*A slight smile.*) Woman's intuition.

WILL. We have no time; come— (WILL *takes* MEG *by the arm and starts.*)

MEG. Please let me go.

WILL. Meg! We have to leave right now, or we may not be able to make it in time—

MEG. Is the execution public?

WILL. No—we are not permitted to attend. But if he's to be taken out of the Tower, he must pass the Landing at the Thames. We can be there waiting—we can see him once more.

MEG. You go, Will. I am remaining here

WILL. Meg!

MEG. Never mind why. I will not make a public spectacle of myself—I can not do it. You go for all of us— (WILL *stands speechless.*) Go on! You have no time— Go!! (WILL *rushes out;* MEG *walks downstage to us:*) For his persistence, William Roper saw Sir Thomas More for the last time, a brief meeting of only a few words. (SIR THOMAS *steps down from the scaffold,* WILL *runs to him:*)

MORE. William—into your care I commend my daughter and—and this, Son Roper— (MORE *awkwardly shoves the book into* WILL'S *hands, and then exits.* WILL *sadly walks back to the study, pressing the book closely to his breast.*)

MEG. William Roper returned to Chelsea; and life went on. (WILL *sits at the table and opens the book. We see him begin to write.*) As for me—the children came to mark the years, both daughters and sons. My sons were sent soon enough away to school, but my daughters remained here with me. I taught them their catechism, and checked behind their ears bi-annually. But I did not teach them Greek—not for them the mystery of the stars, nor the lyricism of math. They grew up to be big healthy women, giggling in chapel, and gossiping at night. They knitted before the fire and dreamed of the inn-keeper's son; and so passed gaily through their days in darkness. And my husband wrote in his study the history of a great man—to spread the light. (MEG *walks to the table where* WILL ROPER, *frozen, has been writing; picking up the book, she finds a page and reads:*) "When Sir Thomas came from the Tower Wharf, his daughter, my wife, desirous to see her father, and to have his final blessing, tarried. As soon as she saw him—after his blessing on her knees reverently received—she pressing in the throng and through the guard ran to him—and there, openly, in the sight of all, embraced him, took him about the neck, and kissed him. Being all ravished with the entire love of her dear father, thus she clung —until forced apart, which made all around weep at the sight. Thus they departed, never seeing each other more on this earth." (MEG *looks at us carefully, with a gently ironic smile that saddens us:*) Here ends the other story—the story of Sir Thomas. For men are martyred in death. . . . But women—women are martyred in life. I lived on, a story never recorded, until at last, I too, departed. My grave was marked with a stone cut by history; but oh, women of my age—could I have chosen, I would lie with you in your unmarked, communal grave—of silence. (MEG *closes the book. The lights dim.*)

CURTAIN

PROPERTY PLOT

ACT ONE
books—on table, center stage
one large prominent book on table
vellum paper on table
quill pens on table
quill can on table
ink wells on table
table, center stage
two chairs for table, center stage
stool for Alice, up left
block for Cromwell, up right
nail pick—Cromwell
muffin or coffeecake—More
willow switch—Alice
scroll—Cromwell

ACT TWO
table, papers, books, etc. as in Act One
wedding veil—Meg
knitting needles, ball of yarn—Alice
folded scrap of paper—Will
brown mug—Alice
piece of paper—Meg

ACT THREE
table, papers, books, etc. as in Act One
bucket—Meg
chancellor's cape—Cromwell
chancellor's medallion—Cromwell
brown shirt with hole, black thread and needle—Alice
scroll—Cromwell

OTHER TITLES AVAILABLE FROM SAMUEL FRENCH

FEMININE ENDING
Sarah Treem

Full Length / Dark Comedy / 3m, 2f / Various, Unit set
Amanda, twenty-five, wants to be a great composer. But at the moment, she's living in New York City and writing advertising jingles to pay the rent while her fiancée, Jack pursues his singing career. So when Amanda's mother, Kim, calls one evening from New Hampshire and asks for her help with something she can't discuss over the phone, Amanda is only too happy to leave New York. Once home, Kim reveals that she's leaving Amanda father and needs help packing. Amanda balks and ends up (gently) hitting the postman, who happens to be her first boyfriend. They spend the night together in an apple orchard, where Amanda tries to tell Billy how her life got sidetracked. It has something to do with being a young woman in a profession that only recognizes famous men. Billy acts like he might have the answer, but doesn't. Neither does Amanda's mother. Or, for that matter, her father. A Feminine Ending is a gentle, bittersweet comedy about a girl who knows what she wants but not quite how to get it. Her parents are getting divorced, her fiancée is almost famous, her first love reappears, and there's a lot of noise in her head but none of it is music. Until the end.

"Darkly comic. *Feminine Ending* has undeniable wit."
- New York Post

"Appealingly outlandish humor."
- The New York Times

"Courageous. The 90-minute piece swerves with nerve and naivete. Sarah Treem has a voice all her own."
- Newsday

SAMUELFRENCH.COM

Lightning Source UK Ltd.
Milton Keynes UK
UKOW031526200412

191168UK00009B/14/P